PRAYING
Through the Scriptures
31 DAYS TO A DEEPER PRAYER LIFE

For those who have little time for
praying on a consistent, regular
basis, and also for those who love
spending much time in prayer
each day.

Esther Wong

Copyright © Esther Wong 2006

Originally published 2006 by Attributes Pte Ltd, 22 Kallang
Avenue, Hong Aik Industrial Building #05-04, Singapore 339413

This edition published 2008 by CWR, Waverley Abbey House,
Waverley Lane, Farnham, Surrey GU9 8EP, UK. Registered Charity
No. 294387. Registered Limited Company No. 1990308.

The right of Esther Wong to be identified as the author of this
work has been asserted by her in accordance with the Copyright,
Designs and Patents Act 1988.

See back of book for list of National Distributors.

Unless otherwise indicated, all Scripture references are taken
from the Holy Bible, New Living Translation, 2004. Copyright ©
1996. Used by permission of Tyndale House Publishers Inc., Carol
Stream, Illinois 60188. All rights reserved.

Other quotations NKJV: New King James Version, © 1982, Thomas
Nelson Inc.

Concept development, editing, design and production by CWR

Cover image: Photodisc
Internal images: Brand X, Creatas, Design Pics, Digital Stock,
Photodisc

Printed in China by 1010 Printing

ISBN: 978-1-85345-473-8

PRAYER is our lifeline to God. Every born-again believer who desires to grow in God understands the significance of having a strong personal prayer life every single day.

Esther Wong has prepared and written a unique and thoughtfully planned one-month devotional filled with biblical verses of praise and adoration to God. She will take you through each day of the month with particular emphasis on certain areas of need in your life. And she will also lead you to pray for others – including loved ones in your family, those in your workplace and for those around the world.

I believe that as you follow through this devotional, your life will be enriched with the goodness of God as you remember His faithfulness in every area of your life. You will be clothed with the power and presence of the Holy Spirit.

Most of all, my prayer is that by using this prayer guide you will grow closer to Jesus and realise how the mercies of God are, indeed, new every morning.

Rev Kong
Honorary Senior Pastor of City Harvest Church, Singapore

IT HAS BEEN A JOY and a privilege to have known Esther and her husband, Rev Canon Dr James Wong, since they first came to CWR to train in the field of Christian counselling. Esther was often seen on her prayer walks in the early hours of the morning around the lake here at Waverley Abbey House.

I am honoured to be working with both Canon James and Esther in bringing CWR's ministry into Singapore in recent years, and now to be able to make available this invaluable aid to extending our prayer lives. I pray it will greatly enhance your prayer life and help you to grow closer to Jesus by praying daily, according to Scripture.

Mick Brooks
Chief Executive, CWR

Acknowledgement

All glory to God for His infinite mercy and love!

I would like to acknowledge and thank the CWR team, Miss Christina Tan for typing, all my prayer partners, and my husband for his love and prayer support.

This book is a tribute to our good friend and encourager, the late Selwyn Hughes, founder of CWR.

Introduction

There was a season in my life when I felt inadequate in my own prayer life, and I echoed the same request that the disciples asked of Jesus: 'Lord, teach us to pray just as John taught his disciples' (Luke 11:1). I needed to be taught how to pray – so I started to read books on the topic of prayer and they were all so inspiring.

'Praying the Word', as shared by a few authors, drew my attention and as I put this into practice, I learned to pray more effectively and with anticipation each day to hear from God through praying with scriptures. Biblical prayers are scriptures prayed back to God. Praying scriptures on a regular basis implants biblical truths into your heart and mind for daily living. I learned the ACTS pattern for daily prayer very early in my Christian life and I have since applied this pattern daily in my prayer time.

The acronym for ACTS is…
A – Adoration
C – Confession
T – Thanksgiving
S – Supplication

Using this formula prevents my mind from wandering and the 'Word for the Day' section has particularly been helpful in listening to the Lord. I find it especially helpful to use this pattern on a bimonthly or quarterly basis – you soon get familiar with those Scripture passages! Each day brings new areas of prayer for personal needs and new themes for the intercessory prayers. It is helpful to keep a journal of your daily prayer time and to look back to see how God moves through your prayers.

Prayer Guide

I would like to share with you some tips on how to begin using this book.

Every prayer time begins by focusing on God Himself, and never on your needs or problems. You reflect on His goodness, grace, holiness, mercy, love, might, power and dominion.

Read the assigned text.

- **Pause:** Pick out the lines that appeal to you – just open your heart to acknowledge the many aspects of God through the assigned text.

- **Journalling:** It is often helpful to jot down your reflections – it is so refreshing to centre on God and not on your problems or needs. Sometimes you may be led to sing an appropriate song in adoration to God. God is GREAT and God is GOOD!

Confession

This is to remind ourselves how we have fallen short

of the glory and character of God. Pray through the text and allow the Holy Spirit to search your soul for forgotten incidents, for being ungracious, for being harsh, legalistic and so on. Unless sin is confessed, our souls are broken down.

Repentance

This section offers a reminder from the Word that you do not justify your sins by blaming others, circumstances etc. You repent and receive forgiveness.

- **Pause/Journalling:** Sometimes you are required to make restitution. Write down what you need to do as a response to your act of repentance. When repenting, consider these two facts:
  1. I am a new creation.
  2. I must change for the better. I have the resources to change from one degree of glory to another, so I choose to change with the help of the Holy Spirit.

Personal Needs

These are prayers which express your dependence on God and your desire to reach a higher level of maturity in your spiritual life.

- **Pause:** Believe that God is listening to your request as you open your heart to Him. Your special concerns are His concerns too. Commit the day's activities to God: 'I will not move unless He goes ahead of me.' Ask for His direction.

- **Journalling:** Record your petitions by jotting them down and note at least one area of growth in your life to rejoice in.

Intercession

Prayers for others focus on their needs and wellbeing. You are standing in the gap for people close to you, those who are just acquaintances or for others that you know little about. Some prayers are 'spiritual warfare prayers' leading to a breakthrough in their lives.

- **Pause:** God is sovereign – He is all knowing, He is all wisdom and He is able to do all things.

- **Journalling:** Jot down names and special concerns. Give thanks for answered prayers. Sometimes God may direct you to change the course of your prayers. Be persevering in prayer, and rejoice in God's wisdom and ability to answer all prayers.

Word for the Day

Read through the text and be open to God's special word for you for that day.

- **Pause:** Read through the words again and meditate on them as an exercise for the day.

- **Journalling:** Note what God has to say and thank Him for speaking to you.

Thanksgiving and Worship

This is an expression of your thanksgiving for who God is and what He has done for you. It is also thanksgiving in anticipation that the God who loves you will deal with your requests wisely. This is faith-building in action.

- **Pause:** Let the Holy Spirit bring to memory some special occasions or events for thanksgiving to the Lord.

- **Journalling:**
  Record an incident when you felt the hand of God was upon a particular situation. Thank Him also when He shows His wisdom and answers your prayer in a different way!

On some days, you may be led to sing songs expressing your joy in thanksgiving.

Prayers to Encourage

These are prayers and statements of Scripture for ending your time of devotion on a high note.

- **Pause:** End on a victory note. This scripture reminds you of the victorious God you have just spoken to! Prayer changes you!

Let me share with you a simple song that I learned in my youth at St Hilda's School:

> *Day by day, dear Lord of Thee*
> *Three things I pray*
> *To see you more clearly*
> *To love you more dearly*
> *To follow you more nearly*
> *Day by day*

'Day by Day'
Words and music by S. Schwartz (taken from the prayer of St Richard of Chichester)

◊ Adoration

'O Sovereign LORD! You made the heavens and earth by your strong hand and powerful arm. Nothing is too hard for you! You show unfailing love to thousands, but you also bring the consequences of one generation's sin upon the next. You are the great and powerful God, the LORD of Heaven's Armies. You have all wisdom and do great and mighty miracles. You see the conduct of all people, and you give them what they deserve.'

Jeremiah 32:17–20

Pause:
Add other thoughts of adoration.

◊ Confession

'The human heart is the most deceitful of all things and desperately wicked. Who really knows how bad it is? But I, the LORD, search all hearts and examine secret motives. I give all people their due rewards according to what their actions deserve.'

Jeremiah 17:9–10

Pause:
Let the Holy Spirit search your heart for wrong secret motives and confess them before the Lord.

11

◊ Words of Repentance

Who can command things to happen without the
LORD's permission? Then why should we, mere
humans, complain when we are punished for our
sins? Instead, let us test and examine our ways. Let
us turn back to the LORD.

Lamentations 3:37,39–40

◊ Prayers for Personal Needs

Pray for ...

- spiritual victory over worldly ambitions
- victory to overcome lustful desires of the flesh
- continuous growth in the Lord
- physical health and strength
- other matters of concern
- prioritising activities for the day

Journalling
Record the
names of those
for whom you
have prayed,
thanking God
for answered
prayers.

◊ Intercession

Pray for ...

- other believers, especially those with whom you
  are in close contact
- your neighbours
- work or ministry associates
- those going through difficult times

Share each other's burdens, and in this way obey the law of Christ.

Galatians 6:2

◊ Word for the Day

If you think you are standing strong, be careful not to fall. The temptations in your life are no different from what others experience. And God is faithful. He will not allow the temptation to be more than you can stand. When you are tempted, he will show you a way out so that you can endure.

1 Corinthians 10:12–13

◊ Thanksgiving and Worship

Give thanks to the LORD and proclaim his greatness. Let the whole world know what he has done. Give thanks to the LORD, for he is good! His faithful love endures forever.

1 Chronicles 16:8,34

⬢ Prayers to Encourage

This I declare about the LORD: He alone is my refuge, my place of safety; he is my God, and I trust him. For he will rescue you from every trap and protect you from deadly disease.

Psalm 91:2–4

⚬ Adoration

O Lord, our Lord, your majestic name fills the earth!
Your glory is higher than the heavens. You have
taught children and infants to tell of your strength,
silencing your enemies and all who oppose you. When
I look at the night sky and see the work of your fingers
– the moon and the stars you set in place – what are
mere mortals that you should think about them,
human beings that you should care for them?
Psalm 8:1–4

Pause:
Note what
further
thoughts you
have on the
wonders of God.

⚬ Confession

That is why the Lord says, 'Turn to me now, while
there is time! Give me your hearts. Come with
fasting, weeping and mourning. Don't tear your
clothing in your grief, but tear your hearts instead.'
Joel 2:12–13

Pause:
Write down
the things you
have done that
indicate you
have turned
away from the
Lord. Ask for
forgiveness
and return
spiritually to
the Lord.

◊ Words of Repentance

Seek the Lord, while you can find him. Call on him now while he is near. Let the wicked change their ways and banish the very thought of doing wrong. Let them turn to the Lord that he may have mercy on them. Yes, turn to our God, for he will forgive generously.

Isaiah 55:6–7

◊ Prayers for Personal Needs

Pray for ...

- a greater awareness of God's creation so as not to pollute the environment through misuse and carelessness
- a grateful heart to Him for being our Provider
- the ability to enjoy divine health and to turn away from activities that are destructive to your wellbeing
- other matters of concern
- prioritising activities for the day

Day 2

◊ Intercession

Pray for …

- all children everywhere
- children whose hearts are far away from the Lord
- children who are sick physically and mentally
- parents who find difficulty in coping with their children
- children at your church and the work among them

◊ Word for the Day

'My thoughts are nothing like your thoughts,' says the LORD. 'And my ways are far beyond anything you could imagine. For just as the heavens are higher than the earth, so are my ways higher than your ways and my thoughts higher than your thoughts.'

Isaiah 55:8–9

◊ Thanksgiving and Worship

The unfailing love of the LORD never ends! His mercies never cease. Great is his faithfulness; his mercies begin afresh each morning. I say to myself, 'The LORD is my inheritance; therefore I will hope in him!'

Lamentations 3:22–24

⬦ Prayers to Encourage

The one thing I ask of the Lord – the one thing I seek most – is to live in the house of the Lord all the days of my life, delighting in the Lord's perfections and meditating in his Temple. For he will conceal me there when troubles come; he will hide me in his sanctuary. He will place me out of reach on a high rock.

Psalm 27:4–5

◊ Adoration

My heart is confident in you, O God; no wonder I can sing your praises with all my heart! Wake up, lyre and harp! I will wake the dawn with my song. I will thank you, LORD, among all the people. I will sing your praises among the nations. For your unfailing love is higher than the heavens. Your faithfulness reaches to the clouds. Be exalted, O God, above the highest heavens. May your glory shine over all the earth.

Psalm 108:1–5

Pause:
Let the Holy Spirit bring further words of adoration for God and record a new song of adoration from this exercise.

Pause:
Reflect on
how you have
dishonoured
God in your
life. You
may want to
record these
sins. Pray for
forgiveness of
these specific
sins.

◊ Confession

[The people] abandoned the God who had made
them; they made light of the Rock of their salvation.

You neglected the Rock who had fathered you; you
forgot the God who had given you birth.

Deuteronomy 32:18

◊ Words of Repentance

Take control of what I say, O Lord, and guard
my lips. Don't let me drift toward evil or take part
in acts of wickedness. Don't let me share in the
delicacies of those who do wrong.

Psalm 141:3–4

◊ Prayers for Personal Needs

Pray for …

- greater faithfulness as a steward of God in the use
  of time, treasure and talent
- a kind, compassionate heart for the poor, needy
  and under-privileged
- other matters of concern
- prioritising activities for the day

◊ Intercession

Pray for …

- those around the world who are poor and in need
- those living below the poverty line
- people in your surrounding region that are needy
- churches working among the poor and needy
- missionaries you know who are working among the poor and needy
- those suffering injustice
- those working in prison ministry

◊ Word for the Day

Then the King will say to those on his right, 'Come, you who are blessed by my Father, inherit the Kingdom prepared for you from the creation of the world. For I was hungry and you fed me. I was thirsty and you gave me a drink. I was a stranger and you invited me into your home. I was naked, and you gave me clothing. I was sick, and you cared for me. I was in prison, and you visited me.'

Matthew 25:34–36

Journalling:
How have you responded to the needy in your midst?

◊ Thanksgiving and Worship

The LORD is merciful and compassionate, slow to get angry and filled with unfailing love. The LORD is good to everyone. He shows compassion on all his creation. All of your works will thank you, LORD, and your faithful followers will praise you. They will speak of the glory of your kingdom; they will give examples of your power.

Psalm 145:8–11

◊ Prayers to Encourage

Light shines on the godly, and joy on those whose hearts are right. May all who are godly rejoice in the LORD and praise his holy name!

Psalm 97:11–12

◊ Adoration

Sing a new song to the LORD! Let the whole earth sing to the LORD! Sing to the LORD; praise his name. Each day proclaim the good news that he saves. Publish his glorious deeds among the nations. Tell everyone about the amazing things he does. Great is the LORD! He is most worthy of praise! He is to be feared above all gods. The gods of the other nations are mere idols, but the LORD made the heavens. Honor and majesty surround him, strength and beauty are in his sanctuary. Worship the LORD in all his holy splendor. Let all the earth tremble before him.

Psalm 96:1–6,9

Pause: Meditate on God's 'glorious deeds'.

23

Pause:
Allow the Holy Spirit to convict you of the 'lurking sins' in your heart, sins known only to God. Confess them to Him.

◊ Confession

How can I know all the sins lurking in my heart? Cleanse me from these hidden faults. Keep your servant from deliberate sins! Don't let them control me. Then I will be free of guilt and innocent of great sin.

Psalm 19.12–13

◊ Words of Repentance

For I recognize my rebellion; it haunts me day and night. Against you, and you alone, have I sinned; I have done what is evil in your sight.

Psalm 51:3–4

◊ Prayers for Personal Needs

Pray for …

- the ability to break free from pursuing ungodly ambitions and from carrying on traditions and practices that are contrary to the Word of God
- freedom from stressful living by allowing God into worrisome circumstances
- a renewed mind regarding the above
- other matters of concern
- prioritising activities for the day

◊ Intercession

Pray for God to 'make known his acts of mercy' to …

- immediate family members
- relatives with whom you are in close contact
- the sick people among you
- those who are living in a backslidden condition

Journalling:
You may want to record some names of people you have been praying for.

◊ Word for the Day

And so, dear brothers and sisters, I plead with you to give your bodies to God because of all he has done for you. Let them be a living and holy sacrifice – the kind he will find acceptable. This is truly the way to worship him. Don't copy the behavior and customs of this world, but let God transform you into a new person by changing the way you think. Then you will learn to know God's will for you, which is good and pleasing and perfect.

Romans 12:1–2

◊ Thanksgiving and Worship

Praise the LORD! For he has heard my cry for mercy. The LORD is my strength and shield. I trust him with all my heart. He helps me, and my heart is filled with joy. I burst out in songs of thanksgiving.

Psalm 28:6–7

◊ Prayers to Encourage

For the LORD God is our sun and our shield. He gives us grace and glory. The LORD will withhold no good thing from those who do what is right. O LORD of Heaven's Armies, what joy for those who trust in you.

Psalm 84:11–12

⬦ Adoration

'Great and marvelous are your works, O Lord God the Almighty. Just and true are your ways, O King of the nations. Who will not fear you, Lord, and glorify your name? For you alone are holy. All nations will come and worship before you, for your righteous deeds have been revealed.'

Revelation 15:3–4

Pause:
'All nations will come and worship you.' Meditate on these words.

⬦ Confession

But if you are bitterly jealous and there is selfish ambition in your heart, don't cover up the truth with boasting and lying. For jealousy and selfishness are not God's kind of wisdom. Such things are earthly, unspiritual, and demonic. For wherever there is jealousy and selfish ambition, there you will find disorder and evil of every kind.

James 3:14–16

Pause:
You might want to note some besetting sins, that is, sins that are hard to get rid of, and confess them to the Lord.

◊ Words of Repentance

Have mercy on me, O God, because of your unfailing
love. Because of your great compassion, blot out the
stain of my sins. Wash me clean from my guilt. Purify
me from my sin. Purify me from my sins and I will be
clean; wash me and I will be whiter than snow.
Psalm 51:1–2,7

◊ Prayers for Personal Needs

Pray for …

- greater discipline in studying the Word of God
- greater love for the Word
- a spirit of revelation and wisdom for living life
  according to the Word
- other matters of concern
- prioritising activities for the day

Journalling:
Which nations
need prayer
urgently?
Note them.

◊ Intercession

Pray for …

- governments: our own, the 'super power countries',
  countries in crisis, and countries at war
- Christians who are in government, especially those
  known to you by name
- the rulers of countries that are opposed to the gospel

- countries in which unbridled greed, corruption and injustice prevail

◊ Word for the Day

The king's heart is in the hand of the LORD, Like the rivers of water; He turns it wherever He wishes. Every way of a man is right in his own eyes, But the LORD weighs the hearts. To do righteousness and justice is more acceptable to the LORD than sacrifice.

Proverbs 21:1–3 (NKJV)

◊ Thanksgiving and Worship

O LORD, I will honor and praise your name, for you are my God. You do such wonderful things. You planned them long ago, and now you have accomplished them.

Isaiah 25:1

◊ Prayers to Encourage

I pray that God, the source of hope, will fill you completely with joy and peace because you trust in him. Then you will overflow with confident hope through the power of the Holy Spirit.

Romans 15:13

But as for me, how good it is to be near God! I have made the Sovereign LORD my shelter, and I will tell everyone about the wonderful things you do.

Psalm 73:28

◊ Adoration

Your unfailing love, O LORD, is as vast as the heavens; Your faithfulness reaches beyond the clouds. Your righteousness is like the mighty mountains, Your justice like the ocean depths. You care for people and animals alike, O LORD. How precious is your unfailing love, O God! All humanity finds shelter in the shadow of your wings. You feed them from the abundance of your own house, letting them drink from your rivers of delights. For you are the fountain of life, the light by which we see.

Psalm 36:5–9

Pause:
Be inspired to further adore Him. Write your own words of adoration.

Pause:
Allow the
Holy Spirit to
shed light on
the 'secrets of
your heart'.

◊ Confession

If we had forgotten the name of our God or spread
our hands in prayer to foreign gods, God would
surely have known it, for he knows the secrets of
every heart.

Psalm 44:20–21

◊ Words of Repentance

Have mercy on me, O God, because of your
unfailing love. Because of your great compassion,
blot out the stain of my sins. Wash me clean from
my guilt. Purify me from my sin.

Psalm 51:1–2

◊ Prayers for Personal Needs

Pray for ...

- sensitivity to the needs of others in your family
- enablement in fulfilling various family roles
  (for example, as a daughter, spouse, parent,
  grandparent, sibling, in-law, aunt, cousin etc)
- personal vocation and ministry
- job fulfilment
- other matters of concern
- prioritising activities for the day

◊ Intercession

Pray for …

- those in full-time Christian work, especially pastors, elders and heads of denominations
- those in full-time Christian work overseas
- your spiritual teachers and mentors
- new Christians
- those undergoing trials and tribulations

◊ Word for the Day

Let the elders who rule well be counted worthy of double honour, especially those who labour in the word and doctrine.

1 Timothy 5:17 (NKJV)

In the same way, you younger men must accept the authority of the elders. And all of you, serve each other in humility, for 'God opposes the proud, but favors the humble.'

1 Peter 5:5

Journalling:
Note some difficulties that need to be overcome in relationships.

◊ Thanksgiving and Worship

Praise the LORD! I will thank the LORD with all my heart as I meet with his godly people. How amazing are the deeds of the LORD! All who delight in him should ponder them. Everything he does reveals his glory and majesty. His righteousness never fails.

Psalm 111:1–3

◊ Prayers to Encourage

All praise to the God and Father of our Lord Jesus Christ. God is our merciful Father and the source of all comfort. He comforts us in all our troubles so that we can comfort others.

2 Corinthians 1:3–4

◊ Adoration

The heavens proclaim the glory of God. The skies
display his craftsmanship. Day after day they continue
to speak; night after night they make him known.
Psalm 19:1–2

'Blessing and glory and wisdom and thanksgiving
and honor and power and strength belong to our
God forever and ever! Amen.'
Revelation 7:12

Then I saw four angels standing at the four corners
of the earth, holding back the four winds so they
did not blow on the earth or the sea, or even on any
tree. And I saw another angel coming from the east,
carrying the seal of the living God. And he shouted
to those four angels, who had been given power to
harm land and sea,
Revelation 7:1–2

Pause:
Look out for
and appreciate
God's creation.
Write down
your thoughts
that arise.

Pause:
Let the Holy
Spirit search
your heart,
your motives
and affections
which have
been controlled
by patterns
of behaviour
established
from your youth.

⬡ Confession

Put me on trial, Lord, and cross-examine me. Test my motives and heart.

Psalm 26:2

Remember, O Lord, your compassion and unfailing love, which you have shown from long ages past. Do not remember the rebellious sins of my youth. Remember me in the light of your unfailing love, for you are merciful, O Lord.

Psalm 25:6–7

⬡ Words of Repentance

Turn to me and have mercy, for I am alone and in deep distress. My problems go from bad to worse. Oh, save me from them all! Feel my pain and see my trouble. Forgive all my sins.

Psalm 25:16–18

For the honor of your name, O Lord, forgive my many, many sins.

Psalm 25:11

◊ Prayers for Personal Needs

Pray for …

- personal revival
- a greater measure of faith to believe in prayer
- a greater measure of obedience to God's Word
- a greater leaning on the Holy Spirit in all activities
- other matters of concern
- prioritising activities for the day

◊ Intercession

Pray for …

- schools and day-care centres
- positive mass media exposure and influence on children
- parents and other care-givers
- those involved in educational policies and institutions
- children's ministries in our churches
- youth ministries throughout the nation

Journalling: Direct your thoughts on how adults contribute to child abuse. Note your areas of concern.

◊ Word for the Day

Who are those who fear the LORD? He will show them the path they should choose. They will live in prosperity and their children will inherit the land.

Psalm 25:12-13

Lord, let these words sink into me: 'And anyone who welcomes a little child like this on my behalf is welcoming me. But if you cause one of these little ones who trusts in me to fall into sin, it would be better for you to have a large millstone tied around your neck and be drowned in the depths of the sea.'
Matthew 18:5–6

◊ Thanksgiving and Worship

Come, let sing to the LORD! Let us shout joyfully to the Rock of our salvation. Let us come to him with thanksgiving. Let us sing psalms of praise to him. For the LORD is a great God, a great King above all gods … Come, let us worship and bow down. Let us kneel before the LORD our maker …
Psalm 95:1–3,6

◊ Prayers to Encourage

God's way is perfect. All God's promises prove true. He is a shield for all who look to him for protection. For who is God except the LORD? Who but our God is a solid rock?
Psalm 18:30–31

⬥ Adoration

The LORD is king! He is robed in majesty. Indeed the LORD is robed in majesty and armed with strength. The world stands firm and cannot be shaken. Your throne, O LORD, has stood from time immemorial. You yourself are from the everlasting past.

Psalm 93:1–2

Pause:
How have you experienced God's majestic power?

⬥ Confession

The LORD's light penetrates the human spirit, exposing every hidden motive.

Proverbs 20:27

People may be pure in their own eyes, but the LORD examines their motives.

Proverbs 16:2

Pause:
Allow the searchlight of God to highlight what displeases Him in your life. Note honestly what God has revealed to you.

◊ Words of Repentance

Forgive me

For our sins are piled up before God and testify against us.

Isaiah 59:12

O Lord…

I will be careful to live a blameless life – when will you come to help me? I will lead a life of integrity in my own home. I will refuse to look at anything vile and vulgar. I hate all who deal crookedly; I will have nothing to do with them. I will reject perverse ideas and stay away from every evil. I will not tolerate people who slander their neighbors. I will not endure conceit and pride!

Psalm 101:2–5

… Help me, Lord.

◊ Prayers for Personal Needs

Pray for …

- greater discipline in studying God's Word
- help in remembering and applying the Word to daily living
- a greater awareness in the area of spiritual warfare
- a greater commitment to grow into spiritual maturity

- a greater boldness in witnessing for the LORD
- other matters of concern
- prioritising activities for the day

◊ Intercession

Pray for …
- those studying in Bible schools and colleges, and people in Bible study classes that they may understand the truth and be obedient to the Word
- those teaching in the above, especially those you know personally
- those who distort the truth of the Word, that they would be prevented from doing further damage to the family of God
- those who have walked away from God
- those facing discouragement in their ministry

◊ Word for the Day

But you must remain faithful to the things you have been taught. You know they are true, for you know you can trust those who taught you … All Scripture is inspired by God and is useful to teach us what is true and to make us realize what is wrong in our lives. It corrects us when we are wrong and teaches us to

Journalling:
How have you treated the Scriptures? How much time and effort have you given to reading the Word?

do what is right. God uses it to prepare and equip his people to do every good work.

2 Timothy 3:14–17

◊ Thanksgiving and Worship

All praise to God, the Father of our Lord Jesus Christ who has blessed us with every spiritual blessing in the heavenly realms because we are united with Christ … So we praise God for the glorious grace he has poured out on us who belong to his dear Son. He is so rich in kindness and grace that he purchased our freedom with the blood of his Son and forgave our sins. He has showered his kindness on us, along with all wisdom and understanding.

Ephesians 1:3,6–8

◊ Prayers to Encourage

Peace be with you, dear brothers and sisters, and may God the Father and the Lord Jesus Christ give you love with faithfulness. May God's grace be eternally upon all who love our Lord Jesus Christ.

Ephesians 6:23–24

Day 9

PRAYING Through the Scriptures

◊ Adoration

Shout with joy to the Lord, all the earth! Worship the Lord with gladness. Come before him, singing with joy. Acknowledge that the Lord is God! He made us, and we are his. We are his people, the sheep of his pasture.

Psalm 100:1–3

Pause:
Sing praise songs as you read the prayer.

◊ Confession

So humble yourselves before God. Resist the devil and he will flee from you. Come close to God, and God will come close to you. Wash your hands, you sinners; purify your hearts, for your loyalty is divided between God and the world. Let there be tears for what you have done.

James 4:7–9

Pause:
Ask the Holy Spirit to zero in on one specific area of your life which needs to be dealt with. What do you intend to do to show the fruit of repentance?

What is causing the quarrels and fights among you? Don't they come from evil desires at war within you?

James 4:1

Don't grumble about each other, brothers and sisters, or you will be judged.

James 5:9

○ Words of Repentance

O Lord, you have examined my heart and know everything about me. You know when I sit down or stand up. You know my thoughts even when I'm far away.

Psalm 139:1–2

Create in me a clean heart, O God. Renew a loyal spirit within me. Do not banish me from your presence, and don't take your Holy Spirit from me.

Psalm 51:10–11

○ Prayers for Personal Needs

Pray for …

- restored relationships with family members, relatives, other believers, friends and those in

authority over you
- the ability to deal with unforgiveness or hurt in any of the above relationships
- other matters of concern
- prioritising activities for the day

Journalling:
Record specific requests.

◊ Intercession

Pray for …
- immediate family members
- healing of broken families within the Church
- Church leaders and their families
- the nation to uphold family values
- family counselling agencies in the country or Church
- those who work in counselling others

◊ Word for the Day

Imitate God, therefore, in everything you do, because you are his dear children. Live a life filled with love, following the example of Christ. He loved us and offered himself as a sacrifice for us …
Ephesians 5:1–2

Those who belong to Christ Jesus have nailed the passions and desires of their sinful nature to his

cross and crucified them there. Since we are living by the Spirit, let us follow the Spirit's leading in every part of our lives. Let us not become conceited, or provoke one another, or be jealous of one another.
Galatians 5:24–26

⬦ Thanksgiving and Worship

Praise the LORD! Give thanks to the LORD, for he is good! His faithful love endures forever. Who can list the glorious miracles of the LORD? Who can ever praise him enough? There is joy for those who deal justly with others and always do what is right.
Psalm 106:1–3

⬦ Prayers to Encourage

Praise the LORD God, the God of Israel, who alone does such wonderful things. Praise his glorious name forever! Let the whole earth be filled with his glory. Amen and Amen!
Psalm 72:18–19

⬦ Adoration

Praise the LORD! Yes, give praise, O servants of the
LORD. Blessed be the name of the LORD now and
forever. Everywhere – from east to west – praise
the name of the LORD. For the LORD is high above
the nations. His glory is higher than the heavens.
Who can be compared with the LORD our God, who
is enthroned on high? He stoops to look down on
heaven and on earth. He lifts the poor from the dust
and the needy from the garbage dump.

Psalm 113:1–7

Pause:
Meditate
on God's
goodness
as seen
around you.

⬦ Confession

LORD, if you kept a record of our sins, who, O LORD
could ever survive? But you offer forgiveness that we
might learn to fear you.

Psalm 130:3–4

Pause:
Ask God to
help you
overcome
the sins that
cripple you
spiritually.

So put to death the sinful earthly things lurking within you. Have nothing to do with sexual immorality, impurity, lust, and evil desires. Don't be greedy, for a greedy person is an idolator …
Colossians 3:5–6

◊ Words of Repentance

Since you have heard about Jesus and have learned the truth that comes from him, throw off your old sinful nature and your former way of life, which is corrupted by lust and deception. Instead, let the Spirit renew your thoughts and attitudes. Put on your new nature, created to be like God – truly righteous and holy.
Ephesians 4:21–24

◊ Prayers for Personal Needs

Pray for …
- a renewed passion for Jesus – ask and believe as you redirect your focus from self to Jesus
- spiritual insight and wisdom in day-to-day living
- victory in spiritual warfare
- self-control and balance in everything you do
- prioritising activities for the day

⬥ Intercession

Pray for …

- Christian writers, publishers and distributors
- people without access to the Bible to have a copy in their hands
- Bible distributors to resistant countries
- Bible Society, Wycliffe Bible Translators, writers of Bible notes and CWR (publishers of *Every Day with Jesus*)
- personal friends who have difficulty in studying/reading the Bible

Journalling: Record how the publishing ministry has helped you progress in your Christian walk. Write down the specific ministries for which you have prayed.

⬥ Word for the Day

Study this Book of Instruction continually. Meditate on it day and night so you will be sure to obey everything written in it. Only then will you prosper and succeed in all you do.

Joshua 1:8

⬥ Thanksgiving and Worship

Your eternal word, O Lᴏʀᴅ, stands firm in heaven. Your faithfulness extends to every generation, as enduring as the earth you created. Your regulations remain true to this day, for everything serves your plans.

Psalm 119:89–91

◊ Prayers to Encourage

Now may the God of peace – who brought up from the dead our Lord Jesus, the great Shepherd of the sheep, and ratified an eternal covenant with his blood – may he equip you with all you need for doing his will. May he produce in you, through the power of Jesus Christ, every good thing that is pleasing to him. All glory to him forever and ever! Amen.

Hebrews 13:20–21

◊ Adoration

Honor the LORD, you heavenly beings; honor the LORD for his glory and strength. Honor the LORD for the glory of his name. Worship the LORD in the splendor of his holiness … The LORD rules over the floodwaters. The LORD reigns as king forever. The LORD gives his people strength. The LORD blesses them with peace.

Psalm 29:1–2,10–11

Pause:
How do you honour the Lord?

◊ Confession

When I refused to confess my sin, my body wasted away, and I groaned all day long. Day and night your hand of discipline was heavy on me. My strength evaporated like water in the summer heat.

Psalm 32:3–4

Pause:
Allow the Holy Spirit to point out some specific sins in your speech, thoughts, actions or attitudes that dishonour the Lord.

◊ Words of Repentance
Lord …
'I will watch what I do and not sin in what I say. I will hold my tongue when the ungodly are around me.'
Psalm 39:1

Create in me a clean heart, O God. Renew a loyal spirit within me. Do not banish me from your presence, and don't take your Holy Spirit from me. Restore to me the joy of your salvation, and make me willing to obey you. Then I will teach your ways to rebels, and they will return to you.
Psalm 51:10–13

◊ Prayers for Personal Needs
Pray for …
- a greater awareness of using your mouth to speak blessings to others
- greater love and compassion for the poor and needy
- a generous spirit given to warmer hospitality towards strangers and foreigners
- an awareness of the presence of a critical or harsh spirit towards others

- other matters of concern
- prioritising activities for the day

◊ Intercession
Pray for …
- any minority groups in your community
- the churches that cater to their needs
- orphanages at home and abroad
- the destitute in our society
- the mentally and emotionally sick

Journalling:
Ask the Holy Spirit to direct you to pray for specific persons and groups of people you can reach out to personally.

◊ Word for the Day
But the wisdom from above is first of all pure. It is also peace loving, gentle at all times and willing to yield to others. It is full of mercy and good deeds. It shows no favoritism and is always sincere. And those who are peacemakers will plant seeds of peace and reap a harvest of righteousness.

James 3:17–18

The Lord protects the foreigners among us. He cares for the orphans and widows, but he frustrates the plans of the wicked.

Psalm 146:9

◊ Thanksgiving and Worship

Give thanks to the LORD, for he is good!

His faithful love endures forever.

Give thanks to the God of gods.

His faithful love endures forever.

Give thanks to the LORD of lords.

His faithful love endures forever.

Give thanks to him who alone does mighty miracles.

His faithful love endures forever.

Give thanks to him who made the heavens so skillfully.

His faithful love endures forever.

Give thanks to him who placed the earth among the waters.

His faithful love endures forever.

Psalm 136:1–6

◊ Prayers to Encourage

May God be merciful and bless us. May his face shine with favor upon us. May your ways be known throughout the earth, your saving power among people everywhere. May the nations praise you, O God. Yes, may all the nations praise you.

⬦ Adoration

Praise the LORD, all you nations. Praise him, all you people of the earth. For he loves us with unfailing love; the LORD's faithfulness endures forever. Praise the LORD!

Psalm 117:1–2

I will exalt you, my God and King, and praise your name forever and ever. I will praise you every day; yes, I will praise you forever. Great is the LORD! He is most worthy of praise! No one can measure his greatness.

Psalm 145:1–3

Pause:
Allow your heart to melt in the presence of the Lord as you lift your voice to praise Him.

Pause:
Read through
this passage
slowly and let
the Holy Spirit
direct you to
any specific sin
on your part.
Let God bathe
you with His
forgiveness.

⭕ Confession

You should also know this … that in the last
days there will be very difficult times. For people
will love only themselves and their money …
They will be unloving and unforgiving; they will
slander others and have no self-control. They will
be cruel and hate what is good. They will betray
their friends, be reckless, be puffed up with pride,
and love pleasure rather than God. They will act
religious, but they will reject the power that could
make them godly.

2 Timothy 3:1–5

⭕ Words of Repentance

'… we have sinned and done wrong. We have
rebelled against you and scorned your commands and
regulations … Lord, you are in the right; but as you
see, our faces are covered with shame … O our God,
hear your servant's prayer! Listen as I plead.'
And forgive me my sins.

Daniel 9:5,7,17

◊ Prayers for Personal Needs
Pray for …
- the manifestation of the fruit of the Holy Spirit in your life: love, joy, peace, patience, kindness, goodness, faithfulness, gentleness and self-control
- your ministry as a servant of the Lord
- strength and restoration if you are discouraged
- other matters of concern
- prioritising activities for the day

◊ Intercession
Pray for the salvation of …
- immediate family members
- relatives
- close friends
- neighbours
- work associates

Journalling: Praise God for His answers to your prayers for these people.

◊ Word for the Day
I pray that from his glorious, unlimited resources he will empower you with inner strength through his Spirit … Your roots will grow down into God's love and keep you strong. May you experience the love of Christ, though it is too great to understand fully.

Then you will be made complete with all the fullness
of life and power that comes from God.

Ephesians 3:16–17,19

○ Thanksgiving and Worship

I give you thanks, O LORD, with all my heart; I
will sing your praises before the gods. I bow before
your holy Temple as I worship. I praise your name
for your unfailing love and faithfulness; for your
promises are backed by all the honor of your name.
As soon as I pray, you answer me; you encourage me
by giving me strength.

Psalm 138:1–3

○ Prayers to Encourage

Now all glory to God, who is able, through his
mighty power at work within us, to accomplish
infinitely more than we might ask or think. Glory
to him in the church and in Christ Jesus through all
generations forever and ever! Amen.

Ephesians 3:20–21

◊ Adoration

Praise God, for …

Christ is the visible image of the invisible God. He existed before anything was created and is supreme over all creation, for through him God created everything in the heavenly realms and on earth. He made the things we can see and the things we can't see – such as thrones, kingdoms, rulers, and authorities in the unseen world. Everything was created through him and for him. He existed before anything else, and he holds all creation together.

Colossians 1:15–17

Pause:
Meditate on the Person of Christ.

◊ Confession

Be careful then dear brothers and sisters. Make sure that your own hearts are not evil and unbelieving, turning you away from the living God. You must warn each other every day, while it is still 'today,' so

Pause:
Have you at any time turned away from righteous living?

that none of you will be deceived by sin and hardened against God.

Hebrews 3:12–13

◊ Words of Repentance

For I recognize my rebellion; it haunts me day and night. Against you, and you alone have I sinned; I have done what is evil in your sight. You will be proved right in what you say, and your judgment against me is just.

Psalm 51:3–4

Do not banish me from your presence, and don't take your Holy Spirit from me. Restore to me the joy of your salvation and make me willing to obey you.

Psalm 51:11–12

◊ Prayers for Personal Needs

Pray for …

- a renewed fervour and love for Jesus
- a greater measure of faith in His Word and Person
- spiritual insight and wisdom to recognise the 'empty' philosophy and high-sounding nonsense that come from human thinking

- strength to remain rooted in Christ
- deliverance from unbelief and 'hardness of heart'
- other matters of concern
- prioritising activities for the day

◊ Intercession
Pray for …
- all believers, especially those in difficult places of work
- people you know who are backsliders
- those whose hearts are hardened against God
- those forced to renounce their faith in Jesus Christ
- worldly Christians within your circle of friends and relatives

◊ Word for the Day
Dear brothers and sisters, if another believer is overcome by some sin, you who are godly should gently and humbly help that person back onto the right path. And be careful not to fall into the same temptation yourself.

Galatians 6:1

Journalling:
You may wish to record the names and lift them up to the Lord.

Don't be misled – you cannot mock the justice of God. You will always harvest what you plant. Those who live only to satisfy their own sinful nature will harvest decay and death from that sinful nature. But those who live to please the Spirit will harvest everlasting life from the Spirit.

Galatians 6:7–8

◊ Thanksgiving and Worship

Let all that I am praise the LORD; with my whole heart, I will praise his holy name … He does not punish us for all our sins; he does not deal harshly with us, as we deserve. For his unfailing love toward those who fear him is as great as the height of the heavens above the earth.

Psalm 103:1,10–11

◊ Prayers to Encourage

Teach me your ways, O LORD, that I may live according to your truth! Grant me purity of heart, so that I may honor you. With all my heart I will praise you, O LORD my God. I will give glory to your name forever, for your love for me is very great. You have rescued me from the depths of death.

Psalm 86:11–13

◊ Adoration

O God, we meditate on your unfailing love as we
worship in your Temple. As your name deserves, O
God, you will be praised to the ends of the earth.
Your strong right hand is filled with victory. Let the
people on Mount Zion rejoice. Let all the towns of
Judah be glad, because of your justice.

Psalm 48:9–11

Pause:
Think of
some of the
victories
that God
has secured
for you.

◊ Confession

Remember, it is sin to know what you ought to do
and then not do it.

James 4:17

If we claim we have no sin, we are only fooling
ourselves and not living in the truth. But if we
confess our sins to him, he is faithful and just
to forgive us our sins and to cleanse us from all

Pause:
This is what is
known as 'a sin
of omission'
(James 4:17).
Let the Holy
Spirit remind
you of this sin.

wickedness. If we claim we have not sinned, we are calling God a liar and showing that his word has no place in our hearts.

1 John 1:8–10

◊ Words of Repentance

… if anyone does sin, we have an advocate who pleads our case before the Father. He is Jesus Christ, the one who is truly righteous.

1 John 2:1

So, Lord, I will let the Holy Spirit guide [my] life. Then [I] won't be doing what [my] sinful nature craves … [I] belong to Christ Jesus and have nailed the passions and desires of [my] sinful nature to his cross and crucified them there.

Galatians 5:16,24

◊ Prayers for Personal Needs

Pray for greater love and right attitude in relating to …

- immediate family members and elderly relatives
- people who intimidate you
- those in authority over you

- people working with you and for you
- other matters of concern
- prioritising activities for the day

◊ **Intercession**

Pray for …
- the elderly sick: that they may find salvation, joy and strength in Jesus
- the caregivers of the elderly and the handicapped
- the family members of the elderly sick
- those in health institutions; that they may fear God and uphold the sanctity of life in the way God intended

◊ **Word for the Day**

Don't be selfish; don't try to impress others. Be humble, thinking of others as better than yourselves. Don't look out only for your own interests, but take an interest in others, too.

Philippians 2:3–4

What good is it, dear brothers and sisters, if you say you have faith but don't show it by your actions? Can that kind of faith save anyone? Suppose you

Journalling: Take time to record your particular areas of concern, perhaps some specific names or institutions.

see a brother or sister who has no food or clothing, and you say, 'Good-bye and have a good day; stay warm and eat well' – but then you don't give that person any food or clothing. What good does that do? So you see, faith by itself isn't enough. Unless it produces good deeds, it is dead and useless.

James 2:14–17

⬥ Thanksgiving and Worship

Praise the LORD, all you who fear him! Honor him … For he has not ignored or belittled the suffering of the needy. He has not turned his back on them, but has listened to their cries for help.

Psalm 22:23–24

⬥ Prayers to Encourage

Now all glory to God, who is able to keep you from falling away and will bring you with great joy into his glorious presence without a single fault. All glory to him who alone is God, our Savior through Jesus Christ our Lord. All glory, majesty, power, and authority are his before all time, and in the present, and beyond all time! Amen.

Jude 24–25

◊ Adoration

Praise the name of God forever and ever, for he has all wisdom and power. He controls the course of world events; he removes kings and set up other kings. He gives wisdom to the wise and knowledge to the scholars. He reveals deep and mysterious things and knows what lies hidden in darkness, though he is surrounded by light.

Daniel 2:20–22

Pause:
Meditate on the awesomeness of our God.

◊ Confession

Put me on trial, Lord, and cross-examine me. Test my motives and my heart. For I am always aware of your unfailing love and I have lived according to your truth.

Psalm 26:2–3

Pause:
Allow the Holy Spirit to show you the wrong motives for your behaviour and allow wrong affections to surface and confess them before the Lord.

◊ Words of Repentance

For the honor of your name, O Lord, forgive my many, many sins.

Psalm 25:11

Please …
Show me the right path, O Lord; point out the road for me to follow. Lead me by your truth and teach me, for you are the God who saves me. All day long I put my hope in you.

Psalm 25:4–5

O Lord, I give my life to you. I trust in you, my God! Do not let me be disgraced, or let my enemies rejoice in my defeat.

Psalm 25:1–2

◊ Prayers for Personal Needs

Pray for …
- your faith to be strengthened as you endure trials and temptations
- personal integrity in dealing with others
- boldness to stand for righteousness
- boldness to share the gospel of Jesus Christ

- other matters of concern
- prioritising activities for the day

◊ Intercession
Pray for ...
- governments and governing bodies
- the United Nations, that God will be sovereign in all decisions
- nations where unbridled greed, corruption and injustice are rampant
- Middle East nations

Journalling:
Obtain relevant information from magazines, bulletins and newspapers, and record your prayers for the areas that capture your attention.

What is the greatest concern for your nation?

◊ Word for the Day
Can unjust leaders claim that God is on their side – leaders whose decrees permit injustice? They gang up against the righteous and condemn the innocent to death.

Psalm 94:20–21

The LORD frustrates the plans of the nations and thwarts all their schemes. But the LORD's plans stand firm forever; his intentions can never be shaken. What joy for the nation whose God is the LORD, whose people he has chosen as his inheritance.

Psalm 33:10–12

◊ Thanksgiving and Worship

The Lord hears his people when they call to him for help. He rescues them from all their troubles. The Lord is close to the brokenhearted; he rescues those whose spirits are crushed. The righteous person faces many troubles, but the Lord comes to the rescue each time.

Psalm 34:17–19

I give you thanks, O Lord, with all my heart; I will sing your praises before the gods. I bow before your holy Temple as I worship. I praise your name for your unfailing love and faithfulness … Every king in all the earth will thank you, Lord, for all of them will hear your words.

Psalm 138:1–2,4

◊ Prayers to Encourage

'May the Lord bless you and protect you. May the Lord smile on you and be gracious to you. May the Lord show you his favor and give you his peace.'

Numbers 6:24–26

◊ Adoration

'O Lᴏʀᴅ, the God of our ancestor Israel, may you be praised forever and ever! Yours, O Lᴏʀᴅ, is the greatness, the power, the glory, the victory, and the majesty. Everything in the heavens and on earth is yours, O Lᴏʀᴅ, and this is your kingdom. We adore you as the one who is over all things. Wealth and honor come from you alone, for you rule over everything. Power and might are in your hand, and at your discretion people are made great and given strength. O our God, we thank you and praise your glorious name!'

1 Chronicles 29:10–13

Pause:
Meditate further on the passage and the reality of God's ownership of us.

Pause:
Let the Holy
Spirit bring
to mind your
specific sins
that need to be
dealt with and
confess them
to the Lord.

⚬ Confession

God looks down from heaven on the entire human race; he looks to see if anyone is truly wise, if anyone seeks God. But no, all have turned away; all have become corrupt. No one does good, not a single one!

Psalm 53:2–3

⚬ Words of Repentance

'We have sinned, done evil and acted wickedly.'

2 Chronicles 6:37

Hear my prayer, O LORD; listen to my plea! Answer me because you are faithful and righteous … Let me hear of your unfailing love each morning, for I am trusting you. Show me where to walk, for I give myself to you.

Psalm 143:1,8

⚬ Prayers for Personal Needs

Pray for …

- strength to trust God in trying circumstances
- the ability to memorise passages of Scripture for comfort and use
- good stewardship of time, talent and treasure

- other matters of concern
- prioritising activities for the day

◊ **Intercession**
Pray for …
- believers who are decision makers
- the courts and law enforcement agencies to have spiritual wisdom and insight and to be free from corruption; that they will fear God more than man

◊ **Word for the Day**

The godly walk with integrity; blessed are their children who follow them. When a king sits in judgment, he carefully weighs all the evidence, distinguishing the bad from the good … The LORD detests double standards; he is not pleased by dishonest scales.

Proverbs 20:7–8,23

I have hidden your word in my heart, that I might not sin against you … Teach me your decrees, O LORD; I will keep them to the end. Give me undertanding and I will obey your instructions; I will put them into practice with all my heart.

Psalms 119:11,33–34

◊ Thanksgiving and Worship

Praise the LORD! I will thank the LORD with all my heart as I meet with his godly people. How amazing are the deeds of the LORD! All who delight in him should ponder them. Everything he does reveals his glory and majesty. His righteousness never fails. He causes us to remember his wonderful works. How gracious and merciful is our LORD!

Psalm 111:1–4

◊ Prayers to Encourage

May the LORD richly bless both you and your children. May you be blessed by the LORD, who made heaven and earth. The heavens belong to the LORD, but he has given the earth to all humanity … But we can praise the LORD both now and forever! Praise the LORD!

Psalm 115:14–16,18

⬧ Adoration

Praise the LORD!
Praise the LORD from the heavens!
  Praise him from the skies!
Praise him, all his angels!
  Praise him, all the armies of heaven!
Praise him, sun and moon!
  Praise him, all you twinkling stars!
Praise him, skies above!
  Praise him, vapors high above the clouds!
Let every created thing give praise to the LORD,
  for he issued his command, and they came
    into being.
He set them in place forever and ever.
  His decree will never be revoked.

Psalm 148:1–6

Pause:
Adore God for
who He is.

Pause:
Ask for mercy for your specific sins, especially in the spoken word.

◊ Confession

Finally, I confessed all my sin to you and stopped trying to hide my guilt. I said to myself, 'I will confess my rebellion to the LORD.' And you forgave me! All my guilt is gone.

Psalm 32:5

◊ Words of Repentance

I said to myself, 'I will watch what I do and not sin in what I say. I will hold my tongue when the ungodly are around me.'

Psalm 39:1

◊ Prayers for Personal Needs

Pray for …

- the ability to speak words of affirmation and encouragement
- courage to speak for God in and out of season
- self-control in the use of your tongue
- wisdom in counselling others
- patience to listen
- other matters of concern
- prioritising activities for the day

◊ Intercession
Pray for …
- those who teach in schools from nursery to secondary school and further education
- Bible schools and seminaries
- small/cell groups
- your local church pastor and those who are in a position to counsel others

Journalling:
What area
of concern
is the Holy
Spirit leading
you to pray
for? Record
some specific
concerns here.

◊ Word for the Day

Indeed, we all make many mistakes. For if we could control our tongues, we would be perfect and could also control ourselves in every other way … In the same way, the tongue is a small thing that makes grand speeches.

James 3:2,5

Wise words satisfy like a good meal; the right words bring satisfaction. The tongue can bring death or life; those who love to talk will reap the consequences.

Proverbs 18:20–21

A quarrelsome wife is as annoying as constant dripping on a rainy day. Stopping her complaints is like trying to stop the wind or trying to hold something with greased hands.

Proverbs 27:15–16

◊ Thanksgiving and Worship

God's way is perfect. All the LORD's promises prove true. He is a shield for all who look to him for protection. For who is God, except the LORD? Who but our God is a solid rock? … You have made a wide path for my feet to keep them from slipping.

Psalm 18:30–31,36

◊ Prayers to Encourage

May the words of my mouth and the meditation of my heart be pleasing to you, O LORD, my rock and my redeemer.

Psalm 19:14

◊ Adoration

All heaven will praise your great wonders,
LORD; myriads of angels will praise you for your
faithfulness. For who in all of heaven can compare
with the LORD? What mightiest angel is anything
like the LORD? The highest angelic powers stand
in awe of God. He is far more awesome than those
who surround his throne. O LORD God of Heaven's
Armies! Where is there anyone as mighty as you,
O LORD? You are entirely faithful.

Psalm 89:5–8

Pause:
Meditate
on the
faithfulness
of God in
relation to
your own
experience.
You may want
to record
an incident
that reminds
you of His
faithfulness.

◊ Confession

O God, you know how foolish I am; my sins cannot
be hidden from you. Don't let those who trust in
you be ashamed because of me, O Sovereign LORD
of Heaven's Armies.

Psalm 69:5–6

Pause:
What are
your hidden
sins? Let the
Holy Spirit
point them
out to you.

◊ Words of Repentance

Search me, O God, and know my heart; test me and know my anxious thoughts. Point out anything in me that offends you, and lead me along the path of everlasting life.

Psalm 139:23–24

◊ Prayers for Personal Needs

Pray for …

- your role as a peacemaker
- your ability to encourage and build others up within the Body of Christ
- finding new areas of ministry to the Body of Christ
- other matters of concern
- prioritising activities for the day

Journalling: Note some areas of concern.

◊ Intercession

Pray for …

- preachers and evangelists and their families
- those involved in para-church ministries
- unity among the churches in activities that bring glory to God
- national committees that unite churches
- greater networking and co-operation among the churches

◊ Word for the Day

How wonderful and pleasant it is, when brothers live together in harmony! For harmony is as precious as the anointing oil that was poured over Aaron's head, that ran down his beard and onto the border of his robe. Harmony is as refreshing as the dew from Mount Hermon that falls on the mountains of Zion. And there the Lord has pronounced his blessing, even life everlasting.

Psalm 133:1–3

Do everything without complaining and arguing, so that no one can criticize you. Live clean, innocent lives as children of God, shining like bright lights in a world full of crooked and perverse people.

Philippians 2:14–15

◊ Thanksgiving and Worship

The Lord is merciful and compassionate, slow to get angry and filled with unfailing love. The Lord is good to everyone. He showers compassion on all his creation.

Psalm 145:8–9

◊ **Prayers to Encourage**

The LORD keeps you from all harm and watches over your life. The LORD keeps watch over you as you come and go, both now and forever.

Psalm 121:7–8

○ Adoration

Come, let us sing to the LORD! Let us shout joyfully to the Rock of our salvation. Let us come to him with thanksgiving. Let us sing psalms of praise to him. For the LORD is a great God, a great King above all gods … Come, let us worship and bow down. Let us kneel before the LORD our maker, for he is our God. We are the people he watches over, the flock under his care.

Psalm 95:1–3,6–7

Pause:
You may want to kneel and bow down in adoration of our God.

○ Confession

O LORD, I give my life to you. I trust in you, my God! Do not let me be disgraced, or let my enemies rejoice in my defeat … For the honor of your name, O LORD, forgive my many, many sins … Feel my pain and see my trouble. Forgive all my sins.

Psalm 25:1–2,11,18

Pause:
Let the Holy Spirit direct you to your areas of shame and guilt.

83

◊ Words of Repentance

Lord …

I will be careful to live a blameless life – when will you come to help me? I will lead a life of integrity in my own home. I will refuse to look at anything vile and vulgar. I hate all who deal crookedly; I will have nothing to do with them. I will reject perverse ideas and stay away from every evil.

Psalm 101:2–4

◊ Prayers for Personal Needs

Pray for …

- a renewed mind so as to be able to present your body as a holy and living sacrifice to God
- growth in holiness
- the fear of God to overcome the fear of man in your life
- a healthy attitude towards money and material possessions
- other matters of concern
- prioritising activities for the day

◊ Intercession

Pray for …

- those who intimidate you
- those whom you have intimidated
- people for whom wealth is their god
- those struggling financially
- people whose faith is weak

◊ Word for the Day

The Lord said …

'My grace is all you need. My power works best in weakness.'

2 Corinthians 12:9

The blessing of the LORD makes a person rich, and he adds no sorrow with it.

Proverbs 10:22

The generous will prosper; those who refresh others will themselves be refreshed.

Proverbs 11:25

Don't wear yourself out trying to get rich. Be wise enough to know when to quit. In the blink of an eye wealth disappears, for it will sprout wings and fly away like an eagle

Proverbs 23:4–5

◊ Thanksgiving and Worship

Give thanks to the LORD, for he is good!
   His faithful love endures forever …
He remembered us in our weakness.
   His faithful love endures forever …
He gives food to every living thing.
   His faithful love endures forever.
Give thanks to the God of heaven.
   His faithful love endures forever.
Psalm 136:1,23,25–26

◊ Prayers to Encourage

Now may the God of peace make you holy in every
way, and may your whole spirit and soul and body
be kept blameless until our Lord Jesus Christ comes
again. God will make this happen, for he who calls
you is faithful.
1 Thessalonians 5:23–24

◊ Adoration

Great is the LORD! He is most worthy of praise! He is to be feared above all gods. The gods of other nations are mere idols, but the LORD made the heavens! Honor and majesty surround him; strength and joy fill his dwelling. O nations of the world, recognize the LORD, recognize that the LORD is glorious and strong. Give to the LORD the glory he deserves! Bring your offering and come into his presence. Worship the LORD in all his holy splendor.

1 Chronicles 16:25–29

Pause: Write down your thoughts on God's glory and strength.

◊ Confession

And so the LORD says, 'These people say they are mine. They honor me with their lips, but their hearts are far from me. And their worship of me is nothing but man-made rules learned by rote.'

Isaiah 29:13

Pause: Confess your sin of hypocrisy.

You spread out our sins before you – our secret sins
– and you see them all!

Psalm 90:8

◊ Words of Repentance

Lord …

Help me abandon my shameful ways; for your
regulations are good.

Psalm 119:39

◊ Prayers for Personal Needs

Pray for …

- a renewed heart to love God more
- greater contentment in life
- sincerity in word and action, that you mean what
  you say and say what you mean
- other matters of concern
- prioritising activities for the day

◊ Intercession
Pray for …
- people who work for charitable organisations
- recipients of charity, that they may have the right attitude and expectation
- genuine compassion for the less fortunate
- widows and orphans in your church

Journalling:
Let the Holy Spirit guide you in your involvement with charitable works. If you are not already involved, how can you help?

◊ Word for the Day
Dear children, let's not merely say that we love each other; let us show the truth by our actions. Our actions will show that we belong to the truth, so we will be confident when we stand before God.
1 John 3:18–19

Yet true godliness with contentment is itself great wealth. After all, we brought nothing with us when we came into the world, and we can't take anything with us when we leave it. So if we have enough food and clothing, let us be content.
1 Timothy 6:6–8

◊ Thanksgiving and Worship
It is good to give thanks to the LORD, to sing praises to the Most High. It is good to proclaim your unfailing love in the morning, your faithfulness in

the evening, accompanied by the ten-stringed harp and the melody of the lyre. You thrill me, Lord, with all you have done for me! I sing for joy because of what you have done.

Psalm 92:1–4

◊ Prayers to Encourage

May the Lord continually bless you from Zion.
May you see Jerusalem prosper as long as you live.
May you live to enjoy your grandchildren.
May Israel have peace!

Psalm 128:5–6

◊ Adoration

O God, we meditate on your unfailing love as we worship in your Temple. As your name deserves, O God, you will be praised to the ends of the earth. Your strong right hand is filled with victory.

Psalm 48:9–10

'Salvation comes from our God who sits on the throne and from the Lamb! … Amen! Blessing and glory and wisdom and thanksgiving and honor and power and strength belong to our God forever and ever! Amen.'

Revelation 7:10,12

Pause:
Express your own thoughts of devotion.

Pause:
Meditate on
the spiritual
meaning of
'my house
lies in ruins'.
What actions
can you take
to redress the
situation?

⦿ Confession

'Why are you living in luxurious houses while my
house lies in ruins? This is what the LORD of Heaven's
Armies says: Look at what's happening to you! You
have planted much but harvest little. You eat but are
not satisfied. You drink but are still thirsty … Your
wages disappear as though you were putting them in
pockets filled with holes!'

Haggai 1:4–6

⦿ Words of Repentance

O God, you know how foolish I am; my sins cannot
be hidden from you … Rescue me from the mud;
don't let me sink any deeper! … Answer my prayers,
O LORD, for your unfailing love is wonderful. Take
care of me, for your mercy is so plentiful.

Psalm 69:5,14,16

⦿ Prayers for Personal Needs

Pray for …

- strength to combat anxious thoughts and
  withstand temptations
- commitment to be actively involved in building
  'God's house', ie doing things for His kingdom

- faithfulness in tithing and giving
- other matters of concern
- prioritising activities for the day

⬦ Intercession

Pray for …

- believers working in the financial sector, that they may have insight and foresight, wisdom and integrity
- people who manage the finances of the church
- believers to be faithful in tithing
- family members who are weak in financial management
- friends in financial difficulty

⬦ Word for the Day

But people who long to be rich fall into temptation and are trapped by many foolish and harmful desires that plunge them into ruin and destruction. For the love of money is the root of all kinds of evil. And some people, craving money, have wandered from the true faith and pierced themselves with many sorrows.

1 Timothy 6:9–10

Journalling:
Jot down reflections on your attitude towards money and wealth.
Do you withhold your money from missions and needy people?

'So don't worry about these things, saying, "What will we eat? What will we drink? What will we wear?" These things dominate the thoughts of unbelievers, but your heavenly Father already knows all your needs. Seek the Kingdom of God above all else, and live righteously, and he will give you everything you need.'

Matthew 6:31–33

◊ Thanksgiving and Worship

I thank You, Lord, that ... this same God who takes care of [Paul] will supply all [our] needs from his glorious riches which have been given to us in Christ Jesus.

Philippians 4:19

◊ Prayers to Encourage

May he remember all your gifts and look favorably on your burnt offerings ... May he grant your heart's desires and make all your plans succeed. May we shout for joy when we hear of your victory and raise a victory banner in the name of our God. May the LORD answer all your prayers.

Psalm 20:3–5

◊ Adoration

'Stand up and praise the LORD your God, for he lives from everlasting to everlasting! … May your glorious name be praised! May it be exalted above all blessing and praise! You alone are the LORD. You made the skies and the heavens and all the stars. You made the earth and the seas and everything in them. You preserve them all, and the angels of heaven worship you.'

Nehemiah 9:5–6

Pause:
Add your own thoughts of adoration.

◊ Confession

The sin of Judah is inscribed with an iron chisel – engraved with a diamond point on their stony hearts and on the corners of their altars.

Jeremiah 17:1

Pause:
Let the Holy Spirit convict you of 'evil ways' that are not pleasing to God.

⚬ Words of Repentance

I confess that we have sinned against you. Yes, even my own family and I have sinned! We have sinned terribly by not obeying the commands, decrees and regulations that you gave us …

Nehemiah 1:6–7

I repent, Lord!

⚬ Prayers for Personal Needs

Pray for …

- sensitivity to sin
- obedience to the Lord's teaching regarding holiness
- wise use of time for kingdom purposes; doing good works, especially in the light of the Lord's second coming
- other matters of concern
- prioritising activities for the day

Journalling:
Allow the Holy Spirit to draw your attention.

⚬ Intercession

Pray for …

- believers who are unaware of the 'urgency of time'
- loved ones under stress

- people with special needs
- salvation of family members
- protection for those working overseas

◊ **Word for the Day**

So be careful how you live. Don't live like fools, but like those who are wise. Make the most of every opportunity in these evil days. Don't act thoughtlessly, but understand what the Lord wants you to do.

Ephesians 5:15–17

The Lord isn't really being slow about his promise, as some people think. No, he is being patient for your sake. He does not want anyone to be destroyed, but wants everyone to repent … And so, dear friends, while you are waiting for these things to happen, make every effort to be found living peaceful lives that are pure and blameless in his sight.

2 Peter 3:9,14

◊ Thanksgiving and Worship

Enter his gates with thanksgiving; go into his courts with praise. Give thanks to him and praise his name. For the LORD is good. His unfailing love continues forever, and his faithfulness contines to each generation.

Psalm 100:4–5

◊ Prayers to Encourage

Now may our Lord Jesus Christ himself and God our Father, who loved us and by his grace gave us eternal comfort and a wonderful hope, comfort you and strengthen you in every good thing you do and say.

2 Thessalonians 2:16–17

◊ Adoration

Let all that I am praise the LORD; with my whole heart, I will praise his holy name. Let all that I am praise the LORD; may I never forget the good things he does for me … The LORD is like a father to his children, tender and compassionate to those who fear him. For he knows how weak we are; he remembers we are only dust … Praise the LORD, you angels, you mighty ones who carry out his plans, listening for each of his commands.

Psalm 103:1–2,13–14,20

Pause:
Mull over the lines that capture your attention. Express any other thoughts of adoration.

◊ Confession

Listen! The LORD's arm is not too weak to save you, nor is his ear too deaf to hear you call. It's your sins that have cut you off from God. Because of your sins, he has turned away and will not listen anymore.

Isaiah 59:1–2

Pause:
Has this been your experience? Note specific sins you are facing as you read these verses and confess them before the Lord.

◊ Words of Repentance

… we know what sinners we are. We know we have rebelled and have denied the Lord. We have turned our backs on our God.

Isaiah 59:12–13

Teach me your ways, O Lord, that I may live according to your truth! Grant me purity of heart, that I may honor you.

Psalm 86:11

◊ Prayers for Personal Needs

Pray for …

- spiritual health, that God may revive your passion for Him and give you spiritual discernment
- emotional health, that you may be cleansed of sins and bondages
- physical health, that you may be disciplined in looking after your body; ask God for healing in any part that is sick
- other matters of concern
- prioritising activities for the day

◊ Intercession
Pray for …
- the physically handicapped
- the mentally and psychologically disadvantaged, especially those who come from poor homes
- the blind and the deaf
- the chronic sick
- the institutions that care for those above; especially for their workers
- caregivers

◊ Word for the Day
Everyone tried to touch [Jesus], because healing power went out from him, and he healed everyone.
Luke 6:19

Are any of you sick? You should call for the elders of the church to come and pray over you, anointing you with oil in the name of the Lord. Such a prayer offered in faith will heal the sick, and the Lord will make you well. And if you have committed any sins, you will be forgiven.
James 5:14–15

Journalling:
Note several persons you are close to, or connected with.

◊ Thanksgiving and Worship

Let [us] praise the LORD for his great love and for the wonderful things he has done for [us]. For he satisfies the thirsty and fills the hungry with good things.

Psalm 107:8–9

He forgives all my sins and heals all my diseases.

Psalm 103:3

◊ Prayers to Encourage

In times of trouble, may the LORD answer your cry. May the name of the God of Jacob keep you safe from all harm. May he send you help from his sanctuary and strengthen you from Jerusalem. May he remember all your gifts and look favorably on your burnt offerings.

May he grant your heart's desires and make all your plans succeed. May we shout for joy when we hear of your victory and raise a victory banner in the name of our God. May the LORD answer all your prayers.

Psalm 20:1–5

◊ Adoration

I love you, LORD; you are my strength. The LORD is my rock, my fortress, and my savior; my God is my rock, in whom I find protection. He is my shield, the power that saves me, and my place of safety. I called on the LORD, who is worthy of praise, and he saved me from my enemies.

Psalm 18:1–3

Pause:
You may want to write out a song expressing your love for the Lord.

◊ Confession

So put to death the sinful, earthly things lurking within you. Have nothing to do with sexual immorality, impurity, lust, and evil desires. Don't be greedy, for a greedy person is an idolater, worshiping the things of this world. Because of these sins, the anger of God is coming.

Colossians 3:5–6

Pause:
What are the things that hinder your commitment to the Lord?

◊ Words of Repentance

Return, O Israel, to the LORD your God. *We will return to the LORD our God* for [our] sins have brought [us] down. [*We will*] Bring [our] confessions and return to the LORD and say to him, 'Forgive all our sins and graciously receive us, so that we may offer you our praises.'

Hosea 14:1–2

◊ Prayers for Personal Needs

Pray for …

- a change in lifestyle if so convicted
- the discovery of new spiritual gifts for ministry
- better stewardship of existing gifts and talents
- diligence to combat idleness and double-mindedness
- other matters of concern
- prioritising activities for the day

Journalling: Record specific concerns as you pray through these points.

◊ Intercession

Pray for …

- churches that are involved in community projects, that God will provide them with opportunities for service, and supply the required resources

- creativity in meeting needs of the community
- transparency in our daily activities within the community

◊ Word for the Day

Since God chose you to be the holy people he loves, you must clothe yourselves with tenderhearted mercy, kindness, humility, gentleness, and patience. Make allowance for each other's faults, and forgive anyone who offends you. Remember, the Lord forgave you, so you must forgive others. Above all, clothe yourselves with love, which binds us all together in perfect harmony. And let the peace that comes from Christ rule in your hearts. For as members of one body you are called to live in peace. And always be thankful.

Colossians 3:12–15

◊ Thanksgiving and Worship

I will thank you, LORD, among all the people. I will sing your praises among the nations. For your unfailing love is as high as the heavens. Your faithfulness reaches to the clouds. Be exalted, O God, above the highest heavens. May your glory shine over all the earth.

Psalm 57:9–11

◊ **Prayers to Encourage**
May we …

… grow in the grace and knowledge of our Lord and Savior Jesus Christ. All glory to him, both now and forever! Amen.

2 Peter 3:18

◊ Adoration

O LORD, our Lord, your majestic name fills the earth! Your glory is higher than the heavens. You have taught children and infants to tell of your strength, silencing your enemies and all who oppose you. When I look at the night sky and see the work of your fingers – the moon and the stars you set in place – what are mere mortals that you should think about them, human beings that you should care for them? ... O LORD, our Lord, your majestic name fills the earth!

Psalm 8:1–4,9

Pause: Dwell on the wonders of the Lord's creation and His love for us.

Pause:
How do you
intend to
deal with
falsehood and
anger? Ask for
forgiveness
if you have
responded in
anger.

◊ Confession

So stop telling lies. Let us tell our neighbors the truth … And 'don't sin by letting anger control you.' Don't let the sun go down while you are still angry, for anger gives a foothold to the devil.
Ephesians 4:25–27

◊ Words of Repentance

LORD …
[I will] be quick to listen, slow to speak, and slow to get angry. Human anger does not produce the righteousness God desires. So [I must] get rid of all the filth and evil in [my life], and humbly accept the word God has planted in [my heart], for it has the power to save [my soul].
James 1:19–21

◊ Prayers for Personal Needs

Pray for …
- growth in the fruit of the Spirit
- courage to stand up for the truth
- consistency in spending time with God
- other matters of concern
- prioritising activities for the day

◊ Intercession

Pray for …

- all teachers of the Word, that their lifestyles are consistent with the Word of God
- Christians as they witness in their places of work
- God to raise up willing mentors among us

◊ Word for the Day

'You are the salt of the earth. But what good is salt if it has lost its flavor? Can you make it salty again? It will be thrown out and trampled underfoot as worthless. You are the light of the world – like a city on a hilltop that cannot be hidden. No one lights a lamp and then puts it under a basket. Instead, a lamp is placed on a stand, where it gives light to everyone in the house. In the same way, let your good deeds shine out for all to see, so that everyone will praise your heavenly Father.'

Matthew 5:13–16

Journalling:
Note down names of people you are praying for.

◊ Thanksgiving and Worship

Since we are receiving a Kingdom that is unshakable, let us be thankful and please God by worshiping him with holy fear and awe. For our God is a devouring fire.

Hebrews 12:28–29

◊ Prayers to Encourage

Now may the God of peace – who brought up from the dead our Lord Jesus, the great Shepherd of the sheep, and ratified an eternal covenant with his blood – may he equip you with all you need for doing his will. May he produce in you, through the power of Jesus Christ, every good thing that is pleasing to him. All glory to him forever and ever! Amen.

Hebrews 13:20–21

◊ Adoration

Come, everyone! Clap your hands! Shout to God with joyful praise! … God has ascended with a mighty shout. The LORD has ascended with trumpets blaring. Sing praises to God, sing praises; sing praises to our King, sing praises! For God is the King over all the earth. Praise him with a psalm! God reigns above the nations, sitting on his holy throne. The rulers of the world have gathered together with the people of the God of Abraham. For all the kings of the earth belong to God. He is highly honored everywhere.

Psalm 47:1,5–9

Pause:
Fix your thoughts on the Lord God, and note how you would glorify Him.

◊ Confession

Now repent of sins and turn to God, so that your sins may be wiped away.

Acts 3:19

Pause:
Are you burdened by the guilt of sin?

... [There are] vulnerable women who are burdened with the guilt of sin and controlled by various desires.
2 Timothy 3:6

◊ Words of Repentance
I will ...
Wash [myself] and be clean! Get [my] sins out of [His] sight. Give up [my] evil ways.
Isaiah 1:16

◊ Prayers for Personal Needs
Pray for ...
- enthusiasm in evangelism; awareness and compassion for the lost
- readiness at all times to communicate the gospel
- the anointing of the Holy Spirit to equip you to serve God
- a greater desire to exercise the gifts of the Holy Spirit
- other matters of concern
- prioritising activities for the day

◊ Intercession

Pray for ...
- backslidden Christians
- other matters of concern
- those working in mass media and communications
- those who work in government institutions

◊ Word for the Day

For God has not given us a spirit of fear and timidity, but of power, love, and self-discipline. So never be ashamed to tell others about our Lord.

2 Timothy 1:7–8

The message of the cross is foolish to those who are headed for destruction! But we who are being saved know it is the very power of God. As the Scriptures say, 'I will destroy the wisdom of the wise and discard the intelligence of the intelligent.'

1 Corinthians 1:18–19

Journalling:
Note some special concerns. Are you lacking enthusiasm in spreading the gospel? Ask God to empower you.

◊ Thanksgiving and Worship

I will praise the LORD at all times. I will constantly speak his praises. I will boast only in the LORD; let all who are helpless take heart. Come, let us tell of the LORD's greatness; let us exalt his name together. I prayed to the LORD, and he answered me. He freed me from all my fears.

Psalm 34:1–4

◊ Prayers to Encourage

For the LORD God is our sun and our shield. He gives us grace and glory. The LORD will withhold no good thing from those who do what is right. O LORD of Heaven's Armies, what joy for those who trust in you.

Psalm 84:11–12

◊ Adoration

'My heart rejoices in the LORD! The LORD has made me strong. Now I have an answer for my enemies; I rejoice because you rescued me. No one is holy like the LORD! There is no one besides you; there is no Rock like our God … For all the earth is the LORD's, and he has set the world in order. He will protect his faithful ones, but the wicked will disppear in darkness. No one will succeed by strength alone.'

1 Samuel 2:1–2,8–9

Pause:
Express joy in the Lord. Name at least one event in which to rejoice.

◊ Confession

Therefore, since we are surrounded by such a huge crowd of witnesses to the life of faith, let us strip off every weight that slows us down, especially the sin that so easily trips us up.

Hebrews 12:1

Pause:
What are the sins that weigh you down?

⬥ Words of Repentance

People who conceal their sins will not prosper,
but if they confess and turn from them, they will
receive mercy.

Proverbs 28:13

… I confess and turn from my sins.

Oh, what joy for those whose disobedience is
forgiven, whose sin is put out of sight! Yes, what joy
for those whose record the LORD has cleared of guilt,
whose lives are lived in complete honesty!

Psalm 32:1–2

⬥ Prayers for Personal Needs

Pray for …

- the ability and willingness to mend all broken
  relationships and the release from bitter thoughts
- the ability to love and forgive
- care to avoid legalism, hasty judgment, prejudice
  and misconception
- other matters of concern
- prioritising activities for the day

⬤ Intercession

Pray for …

- peace in our nation
- co-operation among countries in the region
- countries at war
- Israel and the Middle East

⬤ Word for the Day

What is causing the quarrels and fights among you? Don't they come from the evil desires at war within you? You want what you don't have, so you scheme and kill to get it. You are jealous of what others have, but you can't get it, so you fight and wage war to take it away from them.

James 4:1–2

Don't speak evil against each other, dear brothers and sisters. If you criticize and judge each other, then you are criticizing and judging God's law … So what right do you have to judge your neighbor?

James 4:11–12

Journalling: Note reports of war, turmoil and unrest in the newspapers.

◊ Thanksgiving and Worship

I will thank you, LORD, among all the people. I will sing your praises among the nations. For your unfailing love is higher than the heavens, Your faithfulness reaches to the clouds. Be exalted, O God, above the highest heavens. May your glory shine over all the earth.

Psalm 108:3–5

◊ Prayers to Encourage

The God of peace will soon crush Satan under your feet. May the grace of our Lord Jesus be with you … All glory to the only wise God, through Jesus Christ, forever. Amen.

Romans 16:20,27

◊ Adoration

The earth is the LORD's, and everything in it. The world and all its people belong to him.For he laid the earth's foundations on the seas and built it on the ocean depths … Open up, ancient gates! Open up, ancient doors, and let the King of glory enter. Who is the King of glory? The LORD, strong and mighty; the LORD, invincible in battle. Open up, ancient gates! Open up, ancient doors, and let the King of glory enter. Who is the King of glory? The LORD of Heaven's Armies – he is the King of glory.

Psalm 24:1–2,7–10

Pause: Concentrate on the uniqueness of the Almighty God.

◊ Confession

Since they thought it foolish to acknowledge God, he abandoned them to their foolish thinking and let them do things that should never be done.

Romans 1:28

Pause: Let the Holy Spirit guide you into confessing specific sins.

119

You may think you can condemn such people, but you are just as bad, and you have no excuse!
Romans 2:1

◊ Words of Repentance
[I will] not let sin control the way [I] live; [I will] not give in to sinful desires. [I will] not let any part of [my] body become an instrument of evil to serve sin.
Romans 6:12–13

◊ Prayers for Personal Needs
Pray for ...
- greater sensitivity to sin, especially recurring 'sinful' thoughts and behaviours
- greater awareness of the wiles and tactics of the evil one
- a greater desire to abide by God's Word
- other matters of concern
- prioritising activities for the day

Journalling:
Prayerfully note your concerns.

◊ Intercession
Pray for ...
- believers who continue to live in sin
- new and young Christians to be grounded in the Word

- servants of God who are overtaken by pride and careless living
- relatives and family members

◊ Word for the Day

So we have not stopped praying for you since we first heard about you. We ask God to give you complete knowledge of his will and to give you spiritual wisdom and understanding. Then the way you live will always honor and please the Lord, and your lives will produce every kind of good fruit. All the while, you will grow as you learn to know God better and better.

Colossians 1:9–10

◊ Thanksgiving and Worship

You faithfully answer our prayers with awesome deeds, O God our savior. You are the hope of everyone on earth …

Psalm 65:5

Praise God, who did not ignore my prayer or withdraw his unfailing love from me.

Psalm 66:20

◊ Prayers to Encourage

For the angel of the LORD is a guard; he surrounds
and defends all who fear him … The eyes of the
LORD watch over those who do right; his ears are
open to their cries for help.

Psalm 34:7,15

◊ Adoration

'… Holy, holy, holy is the Lord God, the Almighty – the one who always was, who is and who is still to come.'

Revelation 4:8

'Worthy is the Lamb who was slaughtered – to receive power and riches and wisdom and strength and honor and glory and blessing.'

Revelation 5:12

'Blessing and honor and glory and power belong to the one sitting on the throne and to the Lamb forever and ever.'

Revelation 5:13

… *Amen.*

Pause:
Picture yourself in the throne-room of the living God and, together with the angels, sing this song.

Pause:
Let the Holy Spirit deal with you, fully cleansing you of any remaining passions and desires that are contrary to the will of God.

◊ Confession

Once you were dead because of your disobedience and your many sins. You used to live in sin, just like the rest of the world, obeying the devil – the commander of the powers in the unseen world. He is the spirit at work in the hearts of those who refuse to obey God. All of us used to live that way, following the passionate desires and inclinations of our sinful nature.

Ephesians 2:1-3

◊ Words of Repentance

'You disciplined me severely, like a calf that needs training for the yoke. Turn me again to you and restore me, for you alone are the LORD my God.'

Jeremiah 31:18

◊ Prayers for Personal Needs

Pray for …

- the ability to be still before God instead of a preoccupation with 'busyness'
- release from the 'fear of man'
- submission to the Word of God
- faith to overcome discouragement

- other matters of concern
- prioritising activities for the day

◊ Intercession
Pray for …
- mothers who are stressed
- schoolchildren facing stress
- those who need to travel frequently because of their work
- the out-of-work breadwinners of families that are stressed
- those who are facing financial difficulty

Journalling:
Note names of those you need to pray for.

◊ Word for the Day
Trust in the LORD with all your heart; do not depend on your own understanding. Seek his will in all you do, and he will show you which path to take. Don't be impressed with your own wisdom. Instead, fear the LORD and turn away from evil. Then you will have healing for your body and strength for your bones.

Proverbs 3:5–8

'So don't worry about these things, saying, "What will we eat? What will we drink? What will we wear?" These things dominate the thoughts of unbelievers, but your heavenly Father already knows all your needs. Seek the Kingdom of God above all else, and live righteously, and he will give you everything you need.'

Matthew 6:31-33

⬧ Thanksgiving and Worship

Let them praise the LORD for his great love and for the wonderful things he has done for them. For he satisfies the thirsty and fills the hungry with good things.

Psalm 107:8–9

⬧ Prayers to Encourage

The LORD rules over the floodwaters. The LORD reigns as king forever. The LORD gives his people strength. The LORD blesses them with peace.

Psalm 29:10–11

◊ Adoration

O nations of the world, recognize the LORD;
recognize that the LORD is glorious and strong. Give
the LORD the glory he deserves! Bring your offering
and come into his courts. Worship the LORD in all
his holy splendor. Let all the earth tremble before
him. Tell all the nations, 'The LORD reigns!' The world
stands firm and cannot be shaken. He will judge all
peoples fairly.

Let the heavens be glad, and the earth rejoice! Let
the sea and everything in it shout his praise! Let the
fields and their crops burst out with joy! Let the trees
of the forest rustle with praise.

Psalm 96:7–12

Pause:
Praise God
for showing
His grace
and glory.

Pause:
Are your words and actions prompted by love or self-centred ambitions?

◊ Confession

But if you are bitterly jealous and there is selfish ambition in your heart, don't cover up the truth with boasting and lying … For wherever there is jealousy and selfish ambition, there you will find disorder and evil of every kind.

James 3:14,16

◊ Words of Repentance

Seek the LORD while you can find him. Call on him now while he is near. Let the wicked change their ways and banish the very thought of doing wrong. Let them turn to the LORD that he may have mercy on them. Yes, turn to our God, for he will forgive generously.

Isaiah 55:6–7

◊ Prayers for Personal Needs

Pray for …

- a greater awareness of greed and envy in your life, not justifying your unrighteous acts
- a willingness to forgive when hurt
- other matters of concern
- prioritising activities for the day

◊ Intercession

Pray for …

- believers living and working in difficult situations
- people living in poor nations
- people who suffer from natural disasters
- Christian workers working among them
- Jerusalem and the Middle East

Journalling:
Note who are
of special
concern as
you pray.

◊ Word for the Day

The faithful love of the LORD never ends! His mercies never cease. Great is his faithfulness; his mercies begin afresh each morning. I say to myself, 'The LORD is my inheritance; therefore I will hope in him!' The LORD is good to those who depend on him, to those who search for him. So it is good to wait quietly for salvation from the LORD. It is good for people to submit at an early age to the yoke of his discipline.
Lamentations 3:22–27

So whatever you say, or whatever you do, remember that you will be judged by the law that sets you free.
James 2:12

◊ Thanksgiving and Worship

All of your works will thank you, Lord, and your faithful followers will praise you … The Lord helps the fallen and lifts up those bent beneath their loads. The eyes of all look to you in hope; you give them their food as they need it. When you open your hand, you satisfy the hunger and thirst of every living thing.

Psalm 145:10,14–16

◊ Prayers to Encourage

The Lord himself watches over you! The Lord stands beside you as your protective shade. The sun will not harm you by day, nor the moon at night. The Lord keeps you from all harm and watches over your life. The Lord keeps watch over you as you come and go, both now and forever.

Psalm 121:5–8

◊ Adoration

Lord, there is no one like you! For you are great and your name is full of power. Who would not fear you, O King of nations? That title belongs to you alone. Among all the wise people of the earth and in all the kingdoms of the world, there is no one like you … the God of Israel is no idol! He is the Creator of everything that exists …

Jeremiah 10:6–7,16

Pause:
Acknowledge God's greatness through songs you know.

◊ Confession

Dear children, keep away from anything that might take God's place in your hearts.

1 John 5:21

'… stay away from idols! I am the one who answers your prayers and cares for you. I am like a tree that is always green; all your fruit comes from me.'

Hosea 14:8

Pause:
Let the Holy Spirit convict you of the sin of idolatry.

◊ Words of Repentance

This is what the LORD says: '… my faithless people, come home to me again, for I am merciful. I will not be angry with you forever. Only acknowledge your guilt. Admit that you rebelled against the LORD your God and committed adultery against him by worshiping idols … Confess that you refused to listen to my voice.'

Jeremiah 3:12–13

◊ Prayers for Personal Needs

Pray for …

- strength to resist all temptation
- greater sensitivity to idolatry in your own life
- wisdom and understanding as you read His Word daily
- other matters of concern
- prioritising activities for the day

◊ Intercession

Pray for …

- each of your family members
- the Holy Spirit to give you opportunities to show God's love to any unsaved members of the family

Journalling: Focus on your family, especially those who worship 'idols'.

- restoration in any broken relationship
- any family you know of that may be in distress

◊ Word for the Day

Yes, each of us will give a personal account to God. So let's stop condemning each other. Decide instead to live in such a way that you will not cause another believer to stumble and fall …

For the Kingdom of God is not a matter of what we eat or drink, but of living a life of goodness and peace and joy in the Holy Spirit. If you serve Christ with this attitude, you will please God, and others will approve of you, too. So then, let us aim for harmony in the church and try to build each other up.

Romans 14:12–13,17–19

◊ Thanksgiving and Worship

How great is the goodness you have stored up for those who fear you. You lavish it on those who come to you for protection, blessing them before the watching world. You hide them in the shelter of your presence, safe from those who conspire against them. You shelter them in your presence, far from accusing tongues.

Psalm 31:19–20

◊ Prayers to Encourage

Now all glory to God, who is able, through his mighty power at work within us, to accomplish infinitely more than we might ask or think. Glory to him in the church and in Christ Jesus through all generations forever and ever! Amen.

Ephesians 3:20–21

National Distributors

UK: (and countries not listed below)
CWR, Waverley Abbey House, Waverley Lane, Farnham, Surrey GU9 8EP.
Tel: (01252) 784700 Outside UK (44) 1252 784700

AUSTRALIA: CMC Australasia, PO Box 519, Belmont, Victoria 3216.
Tel: (03) 5241 3288 Fax: (03) 5241 3290

CANADA: David C Cook Distribution Canada, PO Box 98, 55 Woodslee Avenue,
Paris, Ontario N3L 3E5. Tel: 1800 263 2664

GHANA: Challenge Enterprises of Ghana, PO Box 5723, Accra.
Tel: (021) 222437/223249 Fax: (021) 226227

HONG KONG: Cross Communications Ltd, 1/F, 562A Nathan Road, Kowloon.
Tel: 2780 1188 Fax: 2770 6229

INDIA: Crystal Communications, 10-3-18/4/1, East Marredpalli, Secunderabad
– 500026, Andhra Pradesh. Tel/Fax: (040) 27737145

KENYA: Keswick Books and Gifts Ltd, PO Box 10242, Nairobi.
Tel: (02) 331692/226047 Fax: (02) 728557

MALAYSIA: Salvation Book Centre (M) Sdn Bhd, 23 Jalan SS 2/64, 47300 Petaling
Jaya, Selangor. Tel: (03) 78766411/78766797 Fax: (03) 78757066/78756360

NEW ZEALAND: CMC Australasia, PO Box 303298, North Harbour, Auckland
0751. Tel: 0800 449 408 Fax: 0800 449 049

NIGERIA: FBFM, Helen Baugh House, 96 St Finbarr's College Road, Akoka, Lagos.
Tel: (01) 7747429/4700218/825775/827264

PHILIPPINES: OMF Literature Inc, 776 Boni Avenue, Mandaluyong City.
Tel: (02) 531 2183 Fax: (02) 531 1960

SINGAPORE: Alby Commercial Enterprises Pte Ltd, 95 Kallang Avenue #04-00,
AIS Industrial Building, 339420. Tel: (65) 629 27238 Fax: (65) 629 27235

SOUTH AFRICA: Struik Christian Books, 80 MacKenzie Street, PO Box 1144,
Cape Town 8000. Tel: (021) 462 4360 Fax: (021) 461 3612

SRI LANKA: Christombu Publications (Pvt) Ltd, Bartleet House, 65 Braybrooke
Place, Colombo 2. Tel: (9411) 2421073/2447665

TANZANIA: CLC Christian Book Centre, PO Box 1384, Mkwepu Street, Dar es
Salaam. Tel/Fax: (022) 2119439

USA: David C Cook Distribution Canada, PO Box 98, 55 Woodslee Avenue, Paris,
Ontario N3L 3E5, Canada. Tel: 1800 263 2664

ZIMBABWE: Word of Life Books (Pvt) Ltd, Christian Media Centre, 8 Aberdeen
Road, Avondale, PO Box A480 Avondale, Harare. Tel: (04) 333355 or 091301188

For email addresses, visit the CWR website: www.cwr.org.uk

CWR is a Registered Charity – Number 294387

**CWR is a Limited Company registered in England – Registration
Number 1990308**

Day and Residential Courses
Counselling Training
Leadership Development
Biblical Study Courses
Regional Seminars
Ministry to Women
Daily Devotionals
Books and Videos
Conference Centre

Trusted all Over the World

CWR HAS GAINED A WORLDWIDE reputation as a centre of excellence for Bible-based training and resources. From our headquarters at Waverley Abbey House, Farnham, England, we have been serving God's people for over 40 years with a vision to help apply God's Word to everyday life and relationships. The daily devotional *Every Day with Jesus* is read by nearly a million people in more than 150 countries, and our unique courses in biblical studies and pastoral care are respected all over the world. Waverley Abbey House provides a conference centre in a tranquil setting.

For free brochures on our seminars and courses, conference facilities, or a catalogue of CWR resources, please contact us at the following address. CWR, Waverley Abbey House, Waverley Lane, Farnham, Surrey GU9 8EP, UK

Telephone: **+44 (0)1252 784700**
Email: **mail@cwr.org.uk**
Website: **www.cwr.org.uk**

CWR Applying God's Word *to everyday life and relationships*